dissecting hope.

written by: **shweepy.**

cover art: **aishwarya deopujari.**

1

"dissecting hope." is a collection of poems and short stories
inspired by events that occurred in the lives of countless
people
alive and passed, and some that never existed.

it dives into the emotions of the human experience
and how they relate to **hope.**

may you find connection through these words.

homie.

[imperfect] components.

4

verb

love.

loved; loving

: to hold dear

changer of perspective.

to stare *into* your eyes is to stare *into* my life

there's purpose for gravity

and mud

and spots on giraffes

when you smile I experience the very beginning of my life

to the very end of it

one perked up cheek to the other

hearing you cry makes heaven that much more real because

the urge to pray for your peace hits me like a stone from a sling

your gaze makes loyalty become a physical attribute

the curves on your ears make every single word out of my mouth more

thoughtful and precise and the hair on your head persuades the wind to clock in

I wish you were all I saw

when I look in the mirror

when I look out of the window

when I open a book

because even the worst of my memories

become worth it when I look at you

speak.

don't talk to me

speak into me

until i'm blue in the face

I don't need high noon radio
or television or
waiting room coffee or
a bath with salt and colors

your words are my drug of choice

i'll take my fix please.

reaching for you
was like reaching for my phone
and venus at the same time

I was your person

but there were other people

I was your confidant

but you had no secrets

I was your home

but you were a wanderer.

yet here you are
my ultimate muse

despite getting burned, even venus still rotates around the sun
it really is as simple as that smile
that dose of heroine that I found myself capable of producing with a few nervous
antidotes

einstein wouldn't stand a chance
the immaculate dance that smile choreographed was incomprehensible
the power so overwhelming that I can survive off of seeing it from a distance
i'm looking forward to my next fix

broke, not broken hearted.

here is a string bracelet
from me to you
a symbol of my empty pockets
but full heart

drowning in you.

how *far* must I

       dive
to be present in your
          d e p t h s ?
how *long* must I train to hold onto my
              breath?
as my eyes gray out
the sensation of euphoria spreads through my veins
like a california wildfire

then you pull me back up
with the asinine assumption that i'm dead
but it was the first time
i've ever felt alive

I want to be your therapy, your cure, your mason
the sky is blue with the absence of clouds
so your walls must come down

if paris is the city of love
and my heart is the city of healing
let's take a trip
if I dive too deep and find death
it would be the greatest fate in history
in fact,
        I yearn for it

bottled up poison.

i'll fill this vessel
with that feeling
you're like my cure
please start the healing
i'll take all of your potions,

                              please

how do you interpret this?

feast your heart
on a love unrivaled
be weary to touch
you are NOT entitled
for I am sand that
would slip through
your hands
and I am protected
by mother ocean

my hero in all the land.

you see a stranger
I see a best friend

no more exchanging giggles during spontaneous walks alone
but the air is chilly, and we'd rather sit with each other anyway

you see a stranger
I see a wife

my lobster before, my lobster now
and regardless of what you think
it's more clear than ever before.

you see a stranger
I see a hero

storming your normandy was traumatic, but you came out victorious
and we'll deal with the scars together

you see a stranger
I see a mother

a mother, in every sense of the word
a world changer
whose body and mind has evolved into atmospheric levels of beauty and
innovation
a provider of life, a galaxy of love, a laureate of discipline

in the absolute best way possible there is none like you

with no gloves.

my knuckles callused
on this journey to you
but i'd fight the moon
and it's cronies
the night sky
and the stars and clouds
again and again
to experience your light
forever

the fiery truth of it all.

forests in flames
as I inhale smoke
i'll scream your name
and no remorse is felt
for the burning world around us

> heat engulfs body
> as we wear our birthday suits
> what is, the opposite of pain
> you claw your way
> through my back
> hair singed by pleasure
> legs cooked al dente

all this and
the volcanic eruption
still yet to come
but on the brink
of taking this fire
to another level

> we burn together
> different from the rest
> spreading purposely
> flames in forests

jelly rolls and suave.

your hair tickles my face
and I don't like when
the scent of perfectly imperfect
is that close

I love it

the sun came up earlier than expected.

let's swim through clouds together

make people proud together

dance hard out loud together

do what we vowed together

take advantage

of this surge of hope

we so gladly found together

lets turn in early tonight.

here is my life

    don't handle with care

        just lend me your smile

        a swig of your hair

            i'll mirror the sun and

                make mountains my grave

                when it's you and I

                    promise not to behave

puddles are just another opportunity to care for you.

i'll lay my coat over
that puddle for you

but who are we kidding?
we'll jump in it anyway
because making a mESs of things
helps us feel **human**

noun

nostalgia.

nostalgist; nostalgic

: a wistful or excessively sentimental yearning for return to or of some past period or irrecoverable condition

hopeless romantics have it better.

failing to recreate her past, she drinks to forget
or, does she drink to remember?
                    maybe it *depends*.
her mind as frail as a leaf fighting to stay attached to its branch come fall
                understanding that once detached, it can never return

                            are futures *only* for the **hopeless romantics**?

            as she bumbles and hinges her way to the next lover the sky screams at her
                        imploring her to embrace the fresh air all around

how come the birds sound so different then when she was young?
it's almost as if they grew old along side her and,
also yearn for the jolt of life that old breeze provided
                        they want to go back.
try as they may, they'll camp here reluctantly
in this moment,
                        for now.

red pill blue pill, hurry up and choose.

                              the smell of a lover

endorphin or toxin

                             the touch of their lips

exhilarating or venomous

                           the making of a memory

nostalgia or trauma

                           the sign of a life well lived

the most important decision

my success isn't the same as your success.

forehead wrinkled from faces made through manual labor
I built a skyscraper
american dream success, just look at my callused hands
wife happy that things are going as planned
bury the trauma and cheat on my heart with a cocktail
all these blessing but I feel that i've failed
powers that be aren't the powers in me and they all chatter
because *if* we have less things to worry about
we can be better at the things that actually matter

second chances don't come and go.

drown me
drown drown me
just give me time to

<u>think</u>

to reminisce what
could have been
as my heart is on the brink

will I ever be remembered
if not a fight was put up?

ten pounds of feather is heavier than ten pounds of stone.

often times I think about raisins
and how I used to give them to dad when I emptied the trick or treat bag
how I felt so lucky snapping the turkey's wishbone in front of distant cousins at
the dinner table, or
the butterflies dancing in my belly when finding out santa ate the cookies left
out for him, when,
he left a note next to the plate
other times, I beg God to remind me about the everything in between moments
he tells me I can find them in my pillow, where all my other sorrows reside
that pillow knows too much but I keep it because I like excuses and it's thrifted
each feather it's made of holds the weight of another story on its quill
and one day
i'll use each of them to write a book
about remembering everything besides the good ole days

speaking of cookies.

you wouldn't change a thing about your past yet, you've cleared your history, cookies and all.

when yangchen invented the sound of wind.

when you pursue the path
that leads to my past
tell the old me
to embrace the wind
but don't fight back
when he attacks
because the crown he wore
of metal scraps and bottle caps
won't be there anymore
the scars can't be ignored
the hope you bring
he will adore

story time to bore you time.

I sat in a coffee shop in chicago while I fed my baby and behind me sat a
gentleman in a blazer. he seemed anxious. the coffee was strong but nothing to
shake the bones. and it all made sense when a woman walked in and they
exchanged pleasantries. it was a first date. I couldn't help but think that's how
our story started. now I'm at a coffee shop for a different reason, with a new girl.
with our girl. most times, beauty shows up after anxiety.

hang in there.

and the bore continues with continuity.

tasting happiness is but feeling joy
if not for a moment
the way bear feels winter
and you smell fall from the orange leaves

oh to stay in that place
one should not
less desirable would be
an unexpected outcome

our moms are artists.

my mother was an artist
        "dinner is ready!"
                she'd yell from the other room
the exhilaration i'd feel
immeasurable
when she'd demand I say thank you to the nice lady that gave me a candy at
church i'd feel a rush of shyness engulf my body
your favorite movie is land before time and art is subjective
it's emotion
look for it in the tiniest of moments

adjective

sadness.

sadder; saddest

: affected with or expressive of grief or unhappiness

4j & kaboom.

these fingers were nearly g o n e

                      from rubbing puddled eyes

                then you showed up to give their hand a shake

insight and **motivation** drive your **persistent** train of a heart

        beating joyously at the chance to bring me along for the ride

no marble or stone can be carved to represent how solid of an organism you are

fear flees at the sniff of your scent

goals and dreams scream in excitement when your presence is announced

and talking about you like you're *still here* brings all those feelings **back**

                    but it hits everyone differently

                  even the best of them, obviously

        your mirror never showed you what the world saw

           and i'm so sorry

grace was being the bigger person.

when it's right
hard becomes easy
if it's spite
it will hurt deeply

fear and loathing in santa clarita.

crooked vision like hating to love

she always goes back

and we look at her sideways

steal the joy when push comes to shove

there isn't a hack

no avoiding the highways

heavenly Father look down from above

get her back on the track

even if there are byways

the truth hurts.

can a house really be a home? if seeing is believing well, walls can't see. but if
they can talk, would they agree? this must conclude that home is where the
heart is, but what if she's heartless?

> she'd be *dead*, smarty pants

no that's not what it means.

home must be a feeling of comfort

like cinderella felt in her glass shoes
like a phillips screwdriver feels in a drawer of tools
like my arms fit around you

> is this all too soon?

when father explained what home was he never spoke of this
this feeling so complex as all he knew to do was provide

yep, I've got it.

home is what one feels inside
what feels just right

I wish I didn't know, now that I do.

?memories those to tight on hold

with each blink, tears representing memories fall and
i'm taken back

if they reach my neck
they'll be gone forever

but the jar of tears is overflowing, and
it's hard to smile
when you cry.

experiencing happy people in a third world country.

faces of **joy** in
places **destroyed** are
cases that can't be
ignored

your friendly neighborhood reminder to appreciate.

give

   give

     give

I shove cash down a vending machine during lunch break because work is more important than health

the machine is always full from me feeding it, yet I'm never full from what it feeds me

a vicious circle, as my lover fills me with a homemade meal but I fail to fill her with love and attention

and priorities are as straight as the yellow brick road

       give

        give

my lover visits her brother who lives with his mother and ignores all others.

they've had the same couch for decades and insist it's a comfy night's rest. it's not.

           give

praised and adored after just being sold, the couch was indeed comfy.

after years of torture it still gives as best it can.

in return, it takes insults and carries the weight of a family that <u>takes</u>.

my instagram fooled you too?

I scavenge for things

that aren't, *things*

and the rooster crows get quiet

because I live in comfort

but I am not comfortable

when you try to escape reality, try to make it real.

dive bars are the best because they're never loud and you don't have to talk to anyone. you can look down and get lost in the doodles drawn on the bar top. you can create stories for them, live vicariously through their ups and downs, their triumphs and tribulations. mostly their triumphs, though. the escape from reality can feel like a vacation you'd never want to leave, and tapping the wood for a seventh bourbon would buy you another hour on the beach.

she doesn't cry wolf, never.

moon weeps for mother
while she expresses pain
so hiding becomes his sleep
some nights better than others

clouds move along, nervously
waves crash onto land
an attempt to heal with hugs

and humans do their part
their tantrums hide betrayal
until mother kicks the bucket

the war is won.

the war
behind my forehead
is lost
raise your flag
this territory is yours

that mask people put on God.

trying to cure exhaustion is like trying to keep a bandaid on after showering with it. there's always hope it sticks but, it never does. and you complain about traffic and, how there are strays on your head. meanwhile, I scratch my neck seeking that next shot of espresso only to crash moments after having it. and like the sun attacking the clouds in an attempt to shine through, you come at me because it's all I think about, and I don't retaliate because i'm a known coward.

i'm exhausted.

maybe it's because we get most of what we don't want without even trying. maybe it's karma, that mask people put on God. maybe this is normal and the bandaid was never meant to stick

father time.

father, it's time
don't worry, im fine
no longer in prime
no more mountains to climb
no more bottles of wine
no more moments to shine
white flag raised, I resign
please take this as a sign
that i'm in a decline
here, I drew this blurred line
we're no longer aligned
and the father inside
wouldn't bother to try
he would leave you to die
father, it's time
father time
hear my cry

noun

fear.

feared; fearing; fears

: an unpleasant often strong emotion caused by anticipation or awareness of danger

things have really gone too far this time.

sniffing the ground in search of reconciliation
nothing but dust and regret a   p   p e a r
trinkets of days past only resurrect reminders of mistakes that were made
so they get b l o   w   n under the refrigerator with the rest of the bunnies
footprints that kick harder than mules get tears in return
but deserve the baptism
patience wears thin as doing the right thing is leaning towards wrong but
the plot continues to thicken
fighting for what's right now mutates and
the origin of purpose ceases to exist

un*forgettable.*

a *forgiven* sin is not a *forgotten* past
and the church pew only seats so many
when tears dry and spite reacts
fears drive the pain a plenty
don't *forget* what we've been through
please
<u>don't *forget*</u>

don't feel so (spncr) low.

sit here, let's rest
the street light
on it's last leg
flickering but I promise,
it'll shine bright again

i've found comfort
on this same bench
the dark has become
my most hated,
best friend

shh, they're here
they move silently
in the shadows
we must keep that light on
for your life, is a battle

when night comes for seconds
let's welcome it together
since i'll be here
from when you last left

keep to myself until I shouldn't.

are we on the wrong side?

the target is hit

my sweats keep me warm

suddenly

the whole lot is trivial

solace consumes conviction

"in all seriousness" becomes fiction

kids are dead and we carry on

time was then, but now it's now.

stoic in nature the human's corrupt
massaging their fears so all logic **e r u p t s**

what must they do to avoid execution
unite despite contrast with a revolution

contradicting, is it?

brave choices are silent
no attention is gained
an easy world can be violent
but not easily explained

a hero in the making.

pins roll under her skin
and she sells her soul
to what wasn't believed in
when survival seemed slim

darker than the ocean
even darker than her notion
suggests the spirits in her eyes
consuming bitter potions

crickets scream
she steps up most daringly
intentions most caringly
succeeding in awe

she was made for this
but doesn't feel it

vulnerability and fear, and how they align.

clouds cover beauty

when one isn't worthy

and forests get naked

when fighting with winter

so help breathe you in

to avoid all the trouble

you're different than any

i've ever felt before

decisions decisions.

every deep encounter leads to a change within ourselves

one either gains something
invaluable, or loses a piece of themselves so
precious they can't stand the decision they've
made. we must choose our approach to such
encounters with extreme care

make it make sense.

free willy
not the whale, my friend
       he shot an old woman
       but has kids at the den
              I can't make it make sense

it takes two to tango...right?

electricity has been lost

                                        maybe only one side of the home

                        but it seems as if it's out on both

his voltage sporadic

mutating by the hour

when he attempts to suppress the spikes

hope is lost

but when set loose

he loses hope

                        their hands embrace

anticipating a generator strong enough is found

to level out the electricity in their home

                        together

rome if you want to, but every dog has its day.

pleased furor from the masses
bewildered elucidation from the woke

no help from one's glasses
only from which children spoke

how does a burning city inspire
fierce and swift amounts of hope

appreciation in madness
humanity nears its final croak

thank the heavens that there are heavens.

quick sand and
        shifts
the pony neighs are **heavy**
more so than the weight
pulling *down* a chevy

freedom looms in d i s t a n c e
natures mother resistant
her feeding on a bevy
removing from existence

when one doesn't know what to do.

goals demand humanity
to sweeping streets like there's a finish line
where ten thousand feet have a say
but speak not a word
instead they **stomp**
and disappoint

yet dreams *yearn* for soul
to lay in a field
while sunflowers tower over and
pollen from dandelions trickle onto breeze-bathed skin it calls its home
but I sit here
l o a d i n g . . . . .

worse than both other options

noun

anger.

angered; angering

: a strong feeling of displeasure and usually of antagonism

the rubik's cube was easy when it first came out.

"live the life you want", they say
even if it's all fun
and all play
you only have one shot at this
a beautiful life filled with love and bliss

I call bull.

will you pay my bills while I pursue my dreams?
            perhaps provide food for my family, for free?

i've seen things you'll never see

babies starving
beat
begging on their knees
women raped
left for dead
wearing ripped up tees

sometimes I wish I never experienced this world

stood home, in my bed, warm and furled
I understand, though
glass half full, make it through
but who knew that just a few saw the truth

i'd rather pay my dues

life is long.

don't tell me life is short
that there isn't much time
or to enjoy every second
what in my years
walking this earth
could possibly be longer?

my life is the longest thing I have
i'll do what I want with it

stone fruits ain't too bad when they do their part.

we are friends, right?
you take your mirror shots, i'll write my words
let's acknowledge each other's existence until it does us no good
for now, i'll cheer you on
you're doing great, friend

never ending circle of dang.

it never fails

they hate it

well i'm not an old record you can just trade in at a pawn shop
                            but I *am* b r o k e n.
you ever feel so anxious you want to die? that's a silly question...yeah, well, me
too. screaming in my own head while showing dead eyes is not a skill i'm
comfortable with being so good at. though, if america can recover then so can I.
and the streets of new york city still thrive. attitudes are traded like stocks and
here we bicker about how to cook the potatoes for dinner. no, I don't actually
want to die. that's what makes it suck. give me a pill and give me some time, i'll
make it alright. I guess. then maybe they'll see me differently

why aren't I working like I thought I would?

her legs make the surface adorned
with blades of grass
scurrying to wrap around her toes
the wind parts as she struts liberally
a wolf's howl redirects to she
the crux of existence
yet she raises her cry
to the Lord of the sky
brilliant to the naked truth
that her naked truth
won't help overcome her days

bears hibernate because they have to, not because they want to.

showing face is worse than no face showing
like donating to charity for a tax break, the intentions are clear
but who am I to judge?

auntie drowns vibrations with attitude and we gather around the remaining
ripples with our smores like a campfire

it's always water over the bridge because drowning is preferred and the
intentions are clear

what's right and wrong is blurred
but the intentions are clear

humans don't know what the sky knows.

with holes in my sock

I ride in my yacht

with holes in his sock

his toenails will rot

reality will never be real

from where I stand

it was the ref's fault we lost at life.

inconsiderate dust

refocusing attention by attacking nostrils

impolite rain drops

drowning out the waves of focus on freedom

irregular heartbeat

a reminder that it's nothing or nobody else's fault but my own

excuse the excuses

as one finds their way back

carmen san diego inspired the sun.

reading line to line, but still undefined, is this meaning of the color yellow
how **dare** she shine down from the heavens and spew happiness and hope
while slowly crying deceit that s e e p s into our pores
it's no wonder why she leaves us burnt
the butterflies suggest that yellow provides in a relationship
and one needs to take it slowly with her
only a few hours go by and she ends up leaving
like everyone else
will she ever return?

imagine if rohan never showed.

not even our enemies
would wish this upon us
yet they refuse to help

we'll win
but not everyone will get out

verb

joy.

joyed; joying; joys

: the emotion evoked by well-being, success, or good fortune or by the prospect of possessing what one desires

embracing loneliness.

sit on a bench by yourself in switzerland
surrounded by snow capped mountains

and see if your opinions on *loneliness* change

the air fresher than the outfit you wore on your first day of senior year

the sun creating art before your eyes, nourishing you like you nourish those two
plants at home that you call your children

listen to the birds tell you their stories

the **good** *and* **gruesome**

and how they like bread, but only if it's stale

lay with what grass you can find
and compare it to that lover who hates oranges

but loves the color, orange

even though your feet will tire from travel
keep digging those heels in the dirt

after all
flowers bloom for a reason
enjoy them before they **die**

whimsical smells of pie came from the neighbor's house.

the smell of a fresh start comes with a renewed heart
folding clothes never brought such pleasure and
I welcome the critters to pick from the pie off my window sill

you can find what you need in your head.

joyfully enforce sleep to dream
reality currently mediocre
the burden feels light when your eyes are closed
not for a blink but for a slumber
where father is proud
all monetary dilemmas paid in full
and your fur baby blows out 30 candles on their birthday cake

we exist in imagery
eyes closed shut for good reason
a happy time for humanity
with pain consistent only when we go to bed alone

evolution showing its face in ways we don't recognize, AGAIN.

I decided to mimic a plant, such that i'd move based on where the sun took me. turns out the best changes occur when I let nature lead the way. until she doesn't show up. the bees find someone better and send the worms to eat me alive, or there's no rain to hydrate my roots. But in this I know that another plant thrives. so I guess i'm ok with it. I think. right?

and with evolution, comes self-awareness.

these clothes make me feel naked

they don't cover my sorrow, despite the compliments
so I sit under a waterfall to cry because I think too highly of myself to do so in a
shower
except what should be tears rolling down my face, is actually dirt
I don't ask questions, as it's the only thing that seems to make me unique

running away is the best option at this point, so I do
but running for me is actually a terrifyingly slow traipse
and knocking on the door of said traipse is a breeze, begging to have a
conversation

*I open reluctantly and without delay, the wind cleanses my soul like a baptism
in the jordan*

the fresh strawberries that once burned my tongue taste magical again
and colors fill the sound of music
tongueless birds sing opera to me
waves of creativity crash against my unsteady cranium and
the big bad wolf otherwise known as fear dies of respiratory failure

best of all, I begin to cry real tears

oh, and learning from past mistakes, too.

failing to replace
memories of past mistakes
with what I should have done
to save half a face

but smile either way
or live in endless torment
shed light on what should stay
than figuring how to forget

the sum of those parts = joy through healing.

I feel cleaner than a mud bath
I look brighter than the night sky
and I sound sweeter than nails on a chalkboard
my glass is half full

I feel dirty like a swamp
I look like a mummy resurrected
and I sound like a pig at the slaughter
my glass is half empty

I feel free to make decisions
despite the circumstances
and sometimes all of those are ok

(sometimes it can be hard to find, but it's always there. in this case, kindly view the back cover of this book.)

grass over gravel.

I **crawl** because I cannot **walk** any longer
my legs are
    out
        of commission now that fighting to survive has finally taken its toll
the gravel wonders when it can absorb my minerals for good as it watches the
roaches move faster than me across its hardscape

    "why do you go on?" it asks

    "your soul left you 300 miles ago"

I respond with what feels like my last breath

"I need to die somewhere flowers will grow for the bees and the butterflies"

    because the sea still tides and the sun still shines through the rain clouds, and I
        have yet to feed my dog today.

"once this old me dies though, i'll come back to share a beer with you. we can
reminisce about the rough times"

hair will typically grow back.

as my roots grow *d e e p e r*
and my bark sheds to make room for the larger tree within
i'll embrace the present
while the *worms* and the *squirrels* and *birds*
make me their home

big window.

I saw a coyote through my big window today as my wife laid resting on the couch

might as well be a bed

he gazed around for opportunity, then ran off to most likely take it

like my wife did while our newborn slept

the comparison of a coyote seeking open doors like my baby would someday felt

wrong to start thinking about

but the reality that we are all living beings just made sense so I didn't fight it

suddenly I recognized the inception I stumbled upon

like mom and pop shop through another alleyway in barcelona

I love Barcelona

a mother dreaming in front of a big window

perhaps of opportunity

in front of a coyote seeking just that

she dreamt of the end being the beginning.

they were weathered by joy
when life was too perfect
but then found hope
at the end of it all

inspired by our addictions.

these walls I speak of, they arent of

brick   or   **stone**

           or   **cement**

when I say they're up, it's not the last line of defense

leaves are fragile

paper tears

and these walls will fall like rome

because this big bad wolf doesn't quit

he's learning

he's adapting

slow and steady wins the race

but you showed up

and hope has never been so high

so build me up like you built yourself up after he went away

because soon enough, this bottle will take me

like it took him

we need a trip to disney.

my hair is dirty from hunting
for hope throughout the jungle
the monkeys laugh and
throw their hard earned bananas
while the thorns from brush
slice my joy

but in the fifth grade I had dreams that the monkey's were nice, and shared their
bananas

I know it's out there
and i'll find it

the fundamental query.

the street sign stares back at me
as if i know,

who controls these buckling knees
what this heart's intentions are while here
where the rat race will lead my altered reality
when i'll trip over the roots that break through the road
why the insects led me down this footpath

perspective.

a child, clothes filthy and broken, stands outside in the cold, pouring rain.
the wind tickles her nose like her father's laugh once did before it was taken
without her permission
chills ripple throughout her body as she recognizes it is still warmer outside
than in the war torn shack where she sleeps.
she smiles, starving and exhausted
a bright moment in her day
and I curse the world when my uber is one minute late

the frog missed the lily pad.

toes stick out the front of my shoes after falling hard from the bike of success.
it's a ten speed and without thought, I turned it to eleven

the untouched finish line laughs. but the toes stay quiet, choosing to adjust and
keep working in response

what feel like jets in the sky, others pass me by, as they reach their peak. some
turn around and wave with a smile, others turn around and cry in empathy

one turned around and stopped to help. their face blurred by a love more pure
than a mother shares with her child. these toes feel inspired

just the two of us.

they've *traveled*
through galaxies
star hopping
care free
experiencing fantasies
we all
wish to
see since
hope is
reality now
this I
decree in
all my
totality soon
this will
be me

spilled ice.

I dropped more ice cubes on the floor this morning. there's a 50/50 chance my
dog zooms over to eat them, but that didn't happen today,
so
I kicked them under the fridge. I'm not clumsy, my hands just take longer to
wake up than the rest of my body. I wonder if those ice cubes chat with the dust
under there? or maybe they see old friends. well, what remains of them. maybe
they feel abandoned, or cheated out of an opportunity. maybe they longed to
serve their purpose, with pride and joy
or
maybe they knew their inevitable fate. I can't feel sympathy for things so cold,
can I? we shouldn't cry over spilled ice. my hands have woken up at this point
and those ice cubes did have a purpose after all

hope is in her, ready to show itself.

drowning on cloud eight

but what they don't know?

I adapt

gills will grow

then be replaced

because floating isn't in my dna

glimmer that never fades.

come *rummage* through the museum in my brain
the final tour started at stars 'o clock

first stop to the left, you'll notice a photo of four square with childhood friends
I'll never see again, but never forget

following that is the mural of awareness. notice how it's s h o c k e d, and **dark**
in its tone.

and the next artifact is my least favorite; innocence. you'll need a microscope for
viewing pleasure, otherwise you won't see anything there at all

be sure to watch your step as we approach broken dreams on the ground up
ahead. I never got to sweeping that up

you're allowed to take anything you find

except the last jewel, at the end of the exhibit. I call it
"the glimmer of hope"

even mountains took it for dead.

I crawled through the thorns
of a caskets red roses
I heard their minds changing
without any talking

I saw flowers blooming
without any soil
and i'll fight for the freedom
so everyone feels it

final note from the author.

my weapon of choice is a pen. even when the ink spills, the outcome is beautiful. my leather boots are scuffed, shades scratched, his shirt...torn. and the pen still writes. but what comes from a pen that runs out of ink? well, let me tell you.

Made in the USA
Coppell, TX
03 August 2024

35537770R00055